Cover Designed by Brand Navigation, DeAnna Pierce
Interior Designed by Greg Jackson, Thinkpen Design, LLC

ISBN 10: 1-59145-551-0
ISBN 13: 978-1-59145-551-6

Printed in the United States of America

BLESSED
AMONG WOMEN

GOD'S GIFTS TO MOTHERS

THOMAS NELSON PUBLISHERS
Since 1798

Table of Contents

Blessed are you among women, and blessed is the child you will bear!

LUKE 1:42B NIV

THE GIFT OF A CHILD

The tiny fingers, the button toes, the downy, sweet-smelling hair and precious first words—a baby is indeed a wonderful gift. And children are no less a gift as they get older, begin to show more of their unique personalities, and set off to explore the world around them.

The only way to handle these precious gifts is to savor them—laughing together, exchanging hugs and kisses, and playing with our kids. Squeeze the life out of every moment. Enjoy your kids and pray prayers of gratitude for God's amazing gift.

WHEN YOU
LOOK AT YOUR LIFE,
THE GREATEST HAPPINESSES
ARE FAMILY HAPPINESSES.

JOYCE BROTHERS

A Walk in the Park

PATRICIA LORENZ

I remember it as if it happened this morning, even though it was quite a few years ago. A simple thing, really—just a walk with my three-year-old. But I also remember the struggles I was feeling, the gloomy mood I was in, and the dozens upon dozens of things I had to do that day. I definitely did not want to go for a walk.

But it was the first really warm spring day after a long, bitter-cold Wisconsin winter, and Andrew begged me to walk with him to the park. I gave in. It would tire him out and then he would take a nice, long nap, and I could finally get some things done, I reasoned.

Andrew scampered out the door. I practically had to jog to keep up with him. I grumbled for him to slow down, wondering if this walk was a good idea after all.

When we reached the park he squealed, "Let's climb up that hill!"

I stalled. "Andrew, there are too many tall weeds."

"There's a path!" He was halfway up before I could protest again. At the top he started an immediate descent, undaunted by the fact that his three-year-old legs couldn't quite keep up with the steep grade. Before I could caution him toward a slower pace, he'd fallen facedown into the grass, then rolled the length of the hill. I expected tears and loud wails.

Instead I heard, "Hey, Jill, I went up to get a pail of water and I fell down and broke my crown!" His laughter was contagious.

Next he talked me into taking the path into the woods along a small, meandering creek. We walked in silence for awhile, stepping on dry twigs and autumn's leftover brown leaves. He stopped cold. "Gretel, I think we're lost. Did you bring any bread crumbs to drop on the path? What if the wicked witch gets us?"

I tried to keep from laughing as I kept up the drama. "Oh, Hansel, the birds ate all the bread crumbs. You'll have to take care of that witch if we meet her."

We came to the footbridge that spanned the creek. Andrew walked across and back again, then scampered down on the bank underneath the bridge. "Mommy, walk across the bridge."

I obeyed, wondering what he was up to now. All at once came a little voice trying to sound mean and ornery.

"Who's that tramping on my bridge?"

I followed my cue, "It's just the littlest Billy goat gruff. Don't eat me up! My bigger brother is coming next."

Walking home, the early afternoon shadows were taller than we were. "I'm going to step on your nose, Mommy!" He smashed his foot down on my shadow.

"Oh, no you don't!" I jumped up and down on his shadow. He squealed with delight as he chased me halfway home.

We passed a dead squirrel on the side of a busy road. "Why is the squirrel dead, Mommy?"

I launched into a long explanation about cars, darting squirrels, death, afterlife, God, and heaven, hoping to ease his troubled mind.

"That's okay. He's just flat. I'll make him some new legs out of Play Doh. Then he'll be okay. Can I have an apple when we get home?"

Before we crossed the street in front of our house, Andrew put his little hand in mine with an adoring look. A loud "I love you, Mommy!" burst from his heart. I scooped him up and smothered him with kisses and hugs.

At that moment I noticed my black mood had lifted. The fresh air and exercise, coupled with the antics of an inquisitive three-year-old, had turned my gloom-and-doom thoughts into brighter ones. Those little-boy kisses and hugs didn't hurt matters either.

When I'm feeling out of sorts or overwhelmed, I've found that the best prescription is a little fresh air and sunshine—and the company of a wee person I care about. A happy child is the world's greatest medicine. ❀

A merry heart
does good, like medicine.

PROVERBS 17:22

Count Your Blessings

What do you love about being a mother? What do you love about each of your children? Take a minute to think and reflect and write those things down.

Then, find a way to share with your kids just how much you feel privileged to be their mother. Spend some one-on-one time with them or share a special treat together. Find a way to communicate, "I'm glad we're a family." Expressing your gratitude will make you—and your kids—feel even more blessed. ❁

Let all that I am praise the LORD; may I never forget
the good things he does for me. He fills my life with
good things. My youth is renewed like the eagle's!

PSALM 103:2, 5 NLT

MOTHER'S LOVE IS PEACE.
IT NEED NOT BE ACQUIRED,
IT NEED NOT BE DESERVED.

ERICH FROMM

Mommy to You Both

P. JEANNE DAVIS

Very early on an overcast spring morning, my husband, John, and I were awakened by a life-altering telephone call. "It's a boy!" Immediately we recognized the voice of the birth grandmother of our soon-to-be child. We had waited for this moment for a long time.

As John and I drove to the hospital, we barely noticed how dreary and rainy the day was, because for us the sun had broken through the clouds. We couldn't get there fast enough.

You're meant to be my son, I thought as I picked him up in my arms that day. I felt a rush of brand-new emotions, joy swirling and circling in my heart. God had answered our prayer.

First-time parents in our forties, John and I were clueless about taking care of a newborn. I learned so much with our baby from daily experience. But most importantly, Johnny taught us how to feel and think like parents for the first time. We were a happy couple caring for our little one.

And then, fifteen months later, I received the astonishing news that I was pregnant at age forty-eight. There in the doctor's office, my stomach hit the floor as I reeled in disbelief. Later my feelings were a mixture of astonishment coupled with that same joy I felt on the day of Johnny's birth. Eight years ago after surgery related to endometriosis, my gynecologist told me it was not utterly impossible but extremely improbable I would ever carry a child.

"This is truly a miracle!" said my obstetrician. "One for the record books, for sure." Emotion filled her usually even voice.

Now our family was complete.

Today, ten years after the birth of our first son, I know something about being a parent. I bonded with two newborns, and I'm meeting the challenges, frustrations, and triumphs of mothering one day at a time, just like every mother.

Our boys are growing up with the normal amount of sibling rivalry. But I was stunned one day when Joshua tearfully petitioned, "Johnny is adopted, but you gave birth to me. I'm your son." This remark came on the heels of a dispute between him and his brother in which Joshua was the loser. He wanted me to take his side. It never occurred to me I must explain to him his brother's adoption under these circumstances.

Then I remembered the occasion only a few months previous when Johnny told Joshua he was adopted. "I want to be adopted too," Joshua had complained.

His older brother made adoption seem more special. I know Joshua felt some envy.

I longed for that day again. Nevertheless, I had an answer for Joshua right from my heart. "For me, whether I gave birth to your brother is unimportant. God brought you and Johnny to me in His own way. I'm Mommy to you both."

Some of us are biological mothers, adoptive mothers, foster mothers, or stepmothers—or a combination. When we love and nurture the children under our care with a total commitment and treat them like the most important people in our world, we are filling the role of a mother.

A friend said to me just before Joshua's birth, "You're being rewarded now with your own baby because you were willing to adopt."

I knew I didn't need to be compensated. I was blessed already. I have experienced adoption and childbirth, and the connection I feel with my two boys is the same. I'm Mommy to them both. ❀

> *Because of his love, God had already decided*
> *to make us his own children through Jesus Christ.*
>
> EPHESIANS 1:5 NCV

From "Children"

BY HENRY WADSWORTH LONGFELLOW

Come to me, O ye children!
For I hear you at your play,
And the questions that perplexed me
Have vanished quite away.

Ye open the eastern windows,
That look towards the sun,
Where thoughts are singing swallows
And the brooks of morning run.

In your hearts are the birds and the sunshine,
In your thoughts the brooklet's flow,
But in mine is the wind of Autumn
And the first fall of the snow. . . .

Come to me, O ye children!
And whisper in my ear
What the birds and the winds are singing
In your sunny atmosphere.

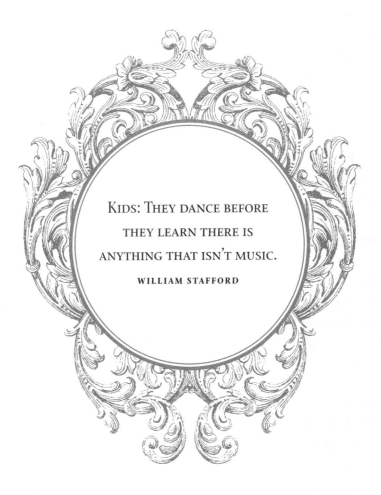

KIDS: THEY DANCE BEFORE
THEY LEARN THERE IS
ANYTHING THAT ISN'T MUSIC.

WILLIAM STAFFORD

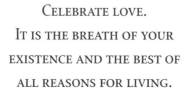

CELEBRATE LOVE.
IT IS THE BREATH OF YOUR
EXISTENCE AND THE BEST OF
ALL REASONS FOR LIVING.

AUTHOR UNKNOWN

Spring Portraits

HEATHER LYNN IVESTER

I remember that glorious spring like it was yesterday. My husband and I lived near a public botanical garden in the middle of the city, and we visited it as often as we could, keeping up with the ever-changing displays of nature.

And that's where I saw them.

It was the most beautiful patch of canary-yellow jonquils I'd ever laid eyes upon. Dozens of blooms, their bright faces basking in the warm March sunshine. That vision of yellow washed over me, and I couldn't get those flowers out of my mind. I dreamed in yellow. I saw everything through yellow-tinted lenses. I felt a desperate passion to do something, anything, to preserve that image of sunshiny splendor.

So I did something a little crazy. Even though we were counting pennies living on a graduate student budget, I splurged on new Easter clothes for our children. I picked out matching yellow seersucker outfits that featured smocked ducklings strutting across the front placket. They were worth every cent.

One weekday morning, I loaded up my son and daughter and drove to the garden, visions of spring portraits dancing in my head. I took the kids and my camera to that jonquil patch and plopped them down in the moist dirt. There was no one else around, so I lost my fear of wondering what others might think of me: a mom with two barefoot kids dressed in Sunday clothes, sitting in the middle of a city-owned plot of blossoms.

I knew I wanted something candid, nothing posed. So I snapped and snapped, using up at least two rolls of film. The kids did what toddlers do best: They touched the flowers, smelled them, waved the stems around a bit. (Okay, so they even picked off a taxpayer-owned petal or two.) Our little photo shoot lasted about twenty minutes, and then it was over.

A few days later, I went back to that spot and noticed the jonquils were not quite at their peak any longer. They looked smaller and leaned over a bit, as if bowing at the end of an extravagant seasonal performance.

Now those pictures mean the world to me. My children are much older, and we've moved away from that city. Yet in a few minutes, I preserved a moment of our lives that I'll always treasure.

How thankful I am that God brought such beauty to my sight. He who created the flowers also created my toddlers, and He allowed me to savor this simple vision of spring. The master gardener loves it when we take time to bask in the beauty He shares with us, celebrating the growth of delicate flowers—and precious little ones. ❦

You give us wine that makes happy hearts
and olive oil that makes our faces shine.
You give us bread that gives us strength.

PSALM 104:15 NCV

God's Promises for Celebrating Our Kids

Behold, children are a heritage from the LORD,
The fruit of the womb is a reward.

PSALM 127:3

Delight yourself also in the LORD,
And He shall give you the desires of your heart.

PSALM 37:4

The children of Your servants will continue,
And their descendants will be established before You.

PSALM 102:28

But as many as received Him, to them He gave the right to
become children of God, to those who believe in His name.

JOHN 1:12

And now abide faith, hope, love, these three; but the greatest of these is love.

1 Corinthians 13:13

THE GIFT OF LOVE

―――――――

Every day, we strive to give our kids the absolute best—we give everything we can to provide for their needs and make them feel safe and loved.

But as much as we give to our kids, the truth is that they are constantly giving to us. They pay us back in smiles and hugs and Mother's Day breakfasts in bed. The love that surges in our hearts for our kids is one of the most life-enriching things we could ever receive.

Every time we look at our family, we know: The love between parents and kids is one of God's greatest gifts.

LET US BE GRATEFUL
TO PEOPLE WHO MAKE
US HAPPY, THEY ARE THE
CHARMING GARDENERS WHO
MAKE OUR SOULS BLOSSOM.

MARCEL PROUST

The Other Mother

MICHELE STARKEY

Realizing that some things are more important than others, I vowed to put a stop to the hurriedness of life and spend one Sunday afternoon with my youngest stepchild. She wanted to play outside on her swing and was begging me to join her. The dust bunnies could run rampant for another day, I decided.

Returning to work on Monday afternoon, I came upon a school crossing guard with her hand poised high in midair. I slowed my car to a stop and watched as the children began crossing the road. One little girl seemed preoccupied with her ponytail, twisting and turning the hair around her small fingers. She stopped in the middle of the road to examine the ends of her long tresses as she slid a finger through them. Several times the guard called to her to "hurry along," and still the little girl kept pace with her own drummer. I chuckled as I watched her skip along.

I knew why this scene was so familiar to me. I have watched it played out many times through the years that she and I have spent together. This child is my husband's youngest daughter, and now she is my daughter too.

Suddenly, she saw me. I watched her little hands waving and heard her voice lifting as she stopped in front of my car. "It's me! It's Annalise." She smiled widely at me as she pointed to herself.

I laughed at how she underestimated my ability to recognize her. I rolled the window down and leaned out. "Hi, honey, I know it's you. Now go across the road toward the crossing guard." She didn't move until the guard approached her and then Annalise stepped closer to my car as though she felt the need to explain to the guard why she'd stopped and who I was but couldn't think of the proper words to describe me.

"She's my . . . it's my . . . that's my . . ." Her face contorted as the guard leaned in a bit closer and prodded, "Come on now, Annalise, we have to get you across the street."

Her defiant little six-year-old spirit wouldn't budge an inch. "But that's my, um . . . she's my *other* mother."

The crossing guard waved at me and took my Annalise by the hand, and I watched through tear-filled eyes as the two of them made the trek safely to the other side of the street. In an instant this youngest daughter of the man I love had defined my new position in life, this unique role with which I'd been blessed. And I knew that this special little girl made that role all the more delightful. I am her "other mother," and I thank God for the title. ❧

Every good gift and every perfect gift is from above,
and comes down from the Father of lights,
with whom there is no variation or shadow of turning.

JAMES 1:17

Love Divine

Paul prayed for the Ephesians, "That you, being rooted and grounded in love, may be able to comprehend with all the saints what is the width and length and depth and height—to know the love of Christ which passes knowledge" (Ephesians 3:17b–19a). The love God has for us is sometimes hard to grasp, and we need His help to understand it.

By giving us children to love, God gives us the opportunity to experience a divine kind of love firsthand. As our Parent, God—

- Tenderly cares for us and leads us (Isaiah 40:11)
- Comforts us (Isaiah 66:13)
- Attends to our needs (Matthew 6:26)
- Gives us loving limits (Hebrews 12:10)
- Sings over us (Zephaniah 3:17)

As much as you love your kids, your Father loves you—and your children—even more. ❦

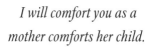

*I will comfort you as a
mother comforts her child.*

ISAIAH 66:13 NLT

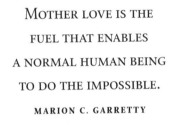

MOTHER LOVE IS THE
FUEL THAT ENABLES
A NORMAL HUMAN BEING
TO DO THE IMPOSSIBLE.

MARION C. GARRETTY

How I Spent My Summer Vacation

PATRICIA LORENZ

On a warm, sunny September day, I said goodbye to my youngest son, Andrew, as he walked toward the jetway to get on a plane bound for Arizona State University to begin his second year of college. I cried a few tears, then forced myself to turn around and walk through the airport and back to my car. I drove home tearfully. *I miss him already!* I whined to myself.

Back at home, I wandered through my empty house recalling the days of what turned out to be our very last summer together. I turned on my computer. Of course the first thing I did was send him a note that would be waiting for him when he returned to the land of cactus, coeds, and college. Later that day, when my inbox filled up with the typical barrage of jokes, quotes, stories, and miscellaneous blather that appear on one's daily e-mail screen, I noticed a quote I'd never seen before. It said, "People will forget what you said. They will forget what you did. But people will never forget how you made them feel."

I thought about how Andrew had made me feel that summer. And I wondered how I'd made him feel.

The previous May, I'd systematically cleared my schedule for most of the summer, trying to avoid any health-and-mind-destroying stress that could easily creep into my life had I been working full time. Andrew was on his way home from his first year of college to have the surgery we hoped could eradicate the disease that had plagued him for nearly three years. His entire colon would be removed and a temporary ostomy bag attached to his side for the next six months. Not the sort of thing a tall, handsome, nineteen-year-old college student looks forward to.

The surgery was successful, but for the first six weeks afterwards he didn't want to see or talk to any of his friends. He just wanted to recuperate. So I was his only conversation partner. By week three I started nagging him daily to go for slow, easy walks with me in the evenings. It was what the doctor ordered, and during those humid treks around the neighborhood I heard about plans he had for a part-time job when he returned to college. I heard about the classes he wanted to take. I heard about the motorcycle he hoped to buy when he returned to the land of high heat and low humidity, about the trips he wanted to take on that motorcycle. He shared the possibilities of what he could do with a German major and wondered aloud what life would be like in his first apartment.

Thinking he should be healing faster, I encouraged him to get out more. "You should be walking more, getting more exercise. You should call your friends, do stuff. It's been four weeks! You should be healed by now. How will you ever be ready to head back to college next month?"

"I'm not ready, Mom. I just don't want to see anyone yet," he said in a quiet voice.

And so, even though professional baseball isn't exactly my favorite pastime, I suggested that Andrew and I go to a Milwaukee Brewers game one evening in July. Baseball is one of Andrew's passions, and sure enough he jumped at the chance.

At Milwaukee County Stadium that night, the game progressed the way most ballgames do. We watched the game, we watched the people, we ate junk food. Then suddenly, just after the seventh inning stretch, there was a power failure and the enormous lights that lit up the field went out. The stadium and field were left in a hazy darkness, and within a few minutes all the players retreated into the dugouts. Because the score was Brewers ten, Kansas City three, many people got up and left for home. Others headed for the refreshment stands, blew bubbles, or sang songs in groups.

When Andrew decided to take a walk around the stadium, I pulled a book out of my backpack and started to read under the few dusky lights that were still on in the grandstand.

Twenty minutes later I looked up to see that the field was aglow with bright lights once again and the game was ready to resume. I couldn't believe my eyes. I hadn't even noticed when the lights came back on. When Andrew got back, he told me they had come on very gradually over the entire thirty-minute period.

Gradually, huh? They went from total darkness to bright enough to play ball, and I hadn't even noticed?

I started to think about Andrew's healing. He'd gone from major surgery to cheering for the Brewers in four weeks and I hadn't really noticed that he'd been getting a little better each day—gradually. I'd been too concerned about pushing him to exercise harder, sleep less, take fewer pain pills, do a few chores, and call his friends to notice that he was walking tall, eating normally, and anxious to get out to see his beloved Brewers.

From that moment on, I let Andrew be in charge of when he would do things around the house or with his friends. My spirits lifted and so did his, and we carried on with our summer.

A few weeks later he started asking questions about cooking. He was planning to move into his first apartment when he returned to school, instead of living in the dorm like the year before. I filled a suitcase with dishes, silverware, pots, pans, and spices and even tucked in two boxes of macaroni and cheese for his first meal in his new apartment.

By the end of the summer my son was healed enough and had enough energy to act like a typical college kid again. He and his friends made it to four or five additional Brewers games, complete with tailgate cooking on a grill before the games.

When I returned home from the airport the day he returned to college, I busied myself cleaning his bedroom and bathroom thoroughly. I put away all the junk a nineteen-year-old boy adds to those rooms in three months' time. I even took down the eight-foot by six-foot Beastie Boys poster that hung over his bed for three years. Since he was planning to stay at ASU the following summer to make up the credits from the classes he had to drop because of his illness, I decided there was no reason to have to look at life-size Beastie Boys each time I walked past his room on the way to my bathroom.

I thought back to our summer of extremes. I recalled the awful hours watching my son fight horrific pain in a hospital after surgery for one whole week. Then it was slow, gentle walks on the bike path in the evenings as we both shared our dreams for the future. His was the world's messiest bathroom for nine weeks—and now one so clean and sparse it seemed to have lost its personality. It was a summer about food, helping him to adjust to a new diet and teaching him how to cook at the same time. It was a summer about love, hugs in the morning and chocolate malts on our way home from the doctors' offices.

After he left I noticed that the house was so quiet that I could hear the leaves falling outside. I thought about that quote. People will forget what you said. They will forget what you did. But people will never forget how you made them feel.

I know neither Andrew nor I will remember everything we said to each other during that summer. And I know we'll both forget a lot of what we did together. But I doubt if we'll ever forget how we made each other feel.

I hope I made him feel safe, well cared for and comfortable during the summer after his surgery. I do know for certain that he made me feel needed and loved. And because of that, I have to say it was the best summer of my life. ❁

Your love has given me great
joy and encouragement.
PHILEMON 1:7A NIV

A MOTHER'S LOVE FOR
HER CHILD IS LIKE NOTHING
ELSE IN THE WORLD. IT KNOWS
NO LAW, NO PITY, IT DARES ALL
THINGS AND CRUSHES DOWN
REMORSELESSLY ALL THAT
STANDS IN ITS PATH.

AGATHA CHRISTIE

*Love suffers long
and is kind; love does not envy;
love does not parade itself, is not puffed up;
does not behave rudely, does not seek its own,
is not provoked, thinks no evil; does not
rejoice in iniquity, but rejoices in the truth;
bears all things, believes all things,
hopes all things, endures all things.*

1 Corinthians 13:4–7

SUDDENLY SHE WAS HERE.
AND I WAS NO LONGER
PREGNANT; I WAS A MOTHER.
I NEVER BELIEVED IN
MIRACLES BEFORE.

ELLEN GREENE

Gifts from My Baby

STEPHANIE WELCHER THOMPSON

One year ago our daughter, Micah Faith, was born. Friends looked at me knowingly and told me that having a baby would change me, but I didn't listen. I was an "older mom," I thought, entering motherhood armed with lots of life experience. How much impact could a baby have on a savvy woman like me?

That attitude faded two days after my husband and I brought Micah home from the hospital. At 4:30 in the afternoon the Wednesday before Thanksgiving, we sat in the emergency room. Our baby had jaundice and the medical staff was considering putting her in the hospital. They weren't sure what to do. Should she be admitted for around-the-clock light treatments, or could we care for her at home? We needed to make the right choice, but we weren't sure what was best. In the stark white hospital room, I knew: My days as a know-it-all were done. I realized that parenting rarely had easy answers or straightforward consequences.

The equipment was delivered to our house. Seeing Micah's five-pound body on the light table for three days was nearly unbearable. Newborns like to be swaddled and cuddled, not lie flat on their backs on an unforgiving table. She flailed her arms and legs, wailing constantly. I cried too. There was nothing to do but pray, talk softly to her, and stroke her head.

Micah eventually recovered and gained weight. By three months, she'd doubled her birth weight. Now a year old, she's a happy, healthy baby.

Some of my favorite times with Micah are when we play. To her, I am the funniest person in the world. We laugh for hours during peek-a-boo and hide-and-seek. In a former life, I planned dinners with friends or went to movies after work. These days, the best entertainment is in my living room, romping on the floor with my daughter.

Motherhood is still uncharted territory. I've survived on "old wives tales," articles from parenting magazines, and the advice of friends and family—all of which seem to conflict. Once we get information, my husband and I pray, then follow our hearts, since we are the ones responsible for raising our daughter and living with the outcome of our decisions.

Despite the uncertainty, I've never had a title that I loved more than "Mommy." Micah began saying "Da

Da" at five months. When we were together, I referred to myself as "Ma Ma." After a few months without results, I countered "Ma Ma" to every "Da Da" she uttered (only when my husband was out of earshot, of course). At eight months, her second words were "baa baa." After a few weeks of hearing "baa baa," I gave in and adopted the moniker for myself.

Finally, at ten months old, she said "Ma Ma" the evening before my birthday. Sweeter than any birthday cake, those words were better than any present. It's still music to my ears when she speaks my new name.

Yes, being a mother has changed me. Who I was and what I did before have little relevance. As we celebrate Micah's first birthday this afternoon, I'll smile secretly to myself. Even though she's opening the presents, I know I'm the one who has been blessed with the real gift. ❀

Don't you see that children are God's best gift?
the fruit of the womb his generous legacy?
PSALM 127:3 THE MESSAGE

God's Promises
for Loving Our Kids

*The father of a good child is very happy; parents
who have wise children are glad because of them.*

PROVERBS 23:24 NCV

*For You, Lord, have made me glad through Your work;
I will triumph in the works of Your hands.*

PSALM 92:4

Fill us with your love every morning.
Then we will sing and rejoice all our lives.

PSALM 90:14 NCV

Whoever receives one little child like
this in My name receives Me.

MATTHEW 18:5

Above all, love each other deeply,
because love covers over a multitude of sins.

1 PETER 4:8 NIV

If any of you lacks wisdom,
let him ask of God,
who gives to all liberally
and without reproach,
and it will be given to him.

JAMES 1:5

THE GIFT OF WISDOM

There are thousands of decisions to make in a day. And while some have more serious consequences than others, we want each one to be the right one; we want the best for our kids in every situation. It can get a little overwhelming—how do we know what to do?

Thankfully, God has given us instincts to follow—and has provided His wisdom for every situation if we will but ask. And one of the sagest elements of maternal wisdom is the recognition that God is in control and wants the best for us and our kids even more than we do.

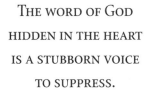

THE WORD OF GOD
HIDDEN IN THE HEART
IS A STUBBORN VOICE
TO SUPPRESS.

BILLY GRAHAM

The Harvest

KAREN MAJORIS GARRISON

It was the perfect summer night to catch fireflies with my children, but my attention snagged on the ailing blueberry bush near our fence. My husband and I had planted it in celebration of the birth of our son, Simeon, but it had never produced fruit.

"Look, Mama!" my son shouted, running towards me. "Fireflies are everywhere!"

I studied his summer wardrobe—bare feet, shorts, and a red baseball cap—and fell in love with motherhood all over again. He spotted a locust shell and inspected it closely. *He's 100% boy*, I grinned, and then I sobered as I remembered the soccer moms talking about their older sons and how rebellious and insensitive they'd become. And recently, a well-intentioned friend had given my husband and me a book on raising boys after her son had left his wife and family for a younger woman. Unsettled by some of the author's statistics, I'd only read the first chapter.

I shivered. Surely our love for Simeon and our commitment to raise him according to Bible principles would shape him and guide him in the ways of the Lord. Still, I was rattled. I needed reassurance. *Help me stay the course, Lord. Help me not to be distracted by worry,* I prayed.

Looking again at the blueberry bush, I noticed brown spots on its foliage. Sighing, I remembered how the previous owners of our home had planted trees to commemorate their children's births. Thinking it a sweet sentiment, my husband and I had continued their tradition and planted a butterfly bush when our daughter, Abigail, arrived.

Her bush had thrived immediately, drawing beautiful winged insects to its purple blossoms. Yet Simeon's blueberry bush struggled to maintain life. I had tried everything, even taking a sample leaf to a renowned gardener, whose business sign cleverly quoted Galatians 6:7: "Whatever you sow, you shall reap."

The gardener's conclusion that the bush had been diseased since we bought it left me despondent. "Don't wait until it dies completely," he suggested. "Pull it out now, and I'll replace it free of charge."

Although a kind offer, I declined. In my maternal reasoning, I imagined that the bush represented Simeon— his trials, dreams, and relationship with his family. And although he and I had an incredible bond, things were changing. He was changing, growing taller and stronger—more independent.

Were the values his sister so eagerly grasped being rooted in him also? Was he developing the godly characteristics necessary to become the best adult, husband, and father he could be later in life?

Burdened by my questions, I stared longingly at the blueberry bush.

But Simeon was oblivious. "I love my bush," he announced, appearing at my side and gently thumbing its leaves. "I call him Blue Boy."

Tears filled my eyes. The bush didn't look as if it would last the summer. I'd better prepare him, I reasoned. "Honey," I began, taking off his baseball hat to kiss his blond head. "Sometimes germs and bad bugs can hurt our plants and make them sick. I think your blueberry bush is sick."

"How do you know?"

"Well," I answered, pointing to the leaves, "one sign of a healthy plant is when it has new leaves. See how its leaves are all dark? New leaves would be a lighter green. There's no new growth here."

"He'll be okay," Simeon reassured me. "Don't worry, Mom. Leave him to me."

I smiled at how he'd decided the bush was a "him" and prayed silently that somehow his bush would survive.

The month of August neared, and over and over again during the evening hours I watched anxiously as Simeon filled up his watering can. He'd been on a mission to cure his blueberry bush, and several times during the day I'd spot him crouched next to its base. Weeks before, he had asked me not to visit his bush until he told me to, and I had agreed with a smile. But my heart was heavy. If the plant died, we'd all be heartbroken.

And then it happened. Early one morning, the kids scurried outside to play. "Mama!" Simeon shouted, running into the kitchen and waving for me to follow him. His face was beaming as we ran toward his bush. "See it? See it?" he panted, pointing to the top of a leaf.

And I did see it. Little pale green leaves, healthier than the bush itself, *growing*.

But I saw other things as well: a picture book, a bottle of perfume, several Band-Aids, and a miscellany of photographs were strewn around the bottom of the bush.

"What is all that?" I asked, curiously fingering the storybook.

Simeon knelt down, handing me the items one by one. "This is the gingerbread man book, the one you said you first read me as a baby. I told it to Blue Boy every day," he boasted. "And this is your vanilla perfume because I love how it smells when I snuggle with you. I sprayed it on him every day too. He loved it."

Sometime after he'd said the words "gingerbread man," tears began to slide down my cheeks.

After making sure my tears were "happy" tears, Simeon continued, "I put a Band-Aid on one of his branches, and trapped a kiss inside just like you do when Sissy and I get hurt." He reached for another book, his pocket-sized Bible. "And I put this near him to comfort him. I can't read too well from it yet, but I don't think he minded. So I just told him Bible stories you and Daddy taught me, and we prayed together too. Just like you and I always do, Mom."

He gathered the pictures, photographs of our family and pets, and handed them to me. "I didn't want him to be lonely at night, so I put all these pictures around him. I remembered what you said about a house being a home only when it's filled with love. So I made him a little home."

He jumped into my lap. "Can you believe it, Mom? It was easy! I just took care of him like you and Daddy take care of me, and now I think he's going to be fine!"

And he was right. The next summer, Blue Boy sprouted a harvest of blossoms, resulting in six ripe blueberries. To celebrate, I promptly made one blueberry pancake that the whole family enjoyed. Simeon beamed with pride, and I thanked God for answering not only my son's prayers, but mine also. In all my concerns about raising children, I'd failed to remember how profound God's promise is: "Whatever a man sows, that he will also reap" (Galatians 6:7b).

That day, I determined to steady my parenting course on the best parenting book of all, the Word of God. Simeon—and his blueberry bush—had helped me see that not only is He the greatest teacher, but also that His love always brings forth an abundant harvest. ❀

The teachings of the Lord are perfect;
they give new strength. The rules of the Lord
can be trusted; they make plain people wise.

PSALM 19:7 NCV

Tricks of the Trade

Is there an aspect of parenting that's troubling you? Are you confused about discipline or nutrition or whether your kids are participating in too many activities? Don't be afraid to seek advice and wisdom. Head to the library and do a little research. Talk to older, wiser moms—your own mom may have all the information you need. Invite a few moms of kids the same age as yours over for snacks one night and listen to their insights.

Most importantly, of course, talk to your heavenly Father, the world's greatest Parent. He will surely provide the wisdom you need, as well as the peace of mind necessary to quell the information overload you might experience. With Him on your side and with your desire to see your kids thrive, you're already well on your way to becoming a savvy mom. ❀

> *The Lord says, "I will make you wise and show you where to go. I will guide you and watch over you."*
>
> PSALM 32:8 NCV

WHEN I STOPPED SEEING
MY MOTHER WITH THE EYES
OF A CHILD, I SAW THE
WOMAN WHO HELPED ME
GIVE BIRTH TO MYSELF.

NANCY FRIDAY

My Mother's Wisdom

AMY SHORE

Throughout the years, my mother has sometimes felt intellectually inferior to the rest of the family she created, because she has the least years logged into higher education. My dad went to college on an accelerated four-years-in-three business program, earning a Bachelor's degree. Then her three children all attended four-year private colleges, each earning Bachelor's degrees in various disciplines. And then each of us went on to earn Master's degrees—me in Humanities, Jon an MBA, and Dan both a law degree and an MBA.

My mother was proud of us as any mother would be, but every now and then she told me wistfully that in a different time and place she would have liked to get a four-year degree, perhaps in nutrition, rather than the two-year Associate's degree in legal secretarial skills she earned from a junior college. I always point out to my mother that she certainly could have earned any degree that she wanted—she was certainly competent enough to persevere through a degree program—but still she stands in awe of those with higher degrees as having accomplished something she could not possibly do.

Today I am here to set the record straight.

My mother has earned a PhD in Life Studies. Rather than spend years poring over notes and scribbling in blue books, she jumped right in and did a parental practicum, one that has lasted almost forty-one years.

As a twenty-two-year-old married only a year, she became a mother to me. She didn't know what she was doing, and she likes to tell me that I was a fat baby because every time I cried, she gave me a bottle. Two years later my brother Jon arrived on the scene, and another two years brought Dan into our family. Before she was twenty-seven years old, my mother was caring for three children all under the age of five—in a three-bedroom house with only one full bathroom.

She planned her days around my father's work schedule because they had only one car. Money was tight, but my mother found a way to make sure we were all fed, clothed, and happy while my father worked hard to support us. Many evenings, after a full day of at-home mommying, even while she was exhausted and craving a little alone time, my mother fed we three hellions dinner while my father was still at work.

There were mornings I remember waving to my dad from the upstairs bedroom window—I hadn't seen him the night before, because I went to bed before he came home from work, and I still had sleep in my eyes when I would catch a glimpse of him leaving for work in those early hours of daybreak. My mother had a lot of responsibility on her young shoulders, and despite living far away from her own mother, she persevered day after day to make our family successful.

My parents were young when they had their children, and they sacrificed a lot in those early years to make sure we had whatever we needed, along with the luxuries of vacations and presents on holidays and birthdays. Now they are enjoying an early retirement in sunny Florida, often catching planes to see their three children and four grandchildren in two different states, soaking up the sunshine, and planning their next vacation.

It is now, after moving from the northeast to the southwest, after dealing with the ups and downs of marriage, after toilet training one and attempting to toilet train another, after a C-section and an adoption journey to Guatemala, and after years and years (and years) of formal classroom education—it is now that I realize that I will be lucky if I can fill my mother's shoes in motherhood and in life.

At night, shortly after my husband Dave returns home from work, when our older daughter, Miranda, is pitching a tirade, trying to complete a difficult homework project, and when our younger daughter, Lucy, is fussy and cranky after a day at preschool, I'm nearly at meltdown stage. I start snapping, and then Dave starts snapping, and then Miranda starts snapping, and soon the four of us are in bad moods going into Lucy's bath time.

It is at those moments of exasperation that I think of how incredible my mother was all those years ago, having dinner on the table (without the luxury of a microwave or a dishwasher) as soon as my father stepped foot into the house from a long day at work, and getting her three little ones into the bathtub and into bed all before eight o'clock. Sure, I remember chaos and my mother's own meltdown moments, but she held it together better than I think I do.

Every morning, I call my mother in Florida. We review what happened in both of our worlds the day and night before, catching up so much that it's as if she lives right next door and not miles and miles away. More often than not, my mother sighs a "been there, done that" sigh when

I recount with horror the craziness at night that hits my house like a tornado, that sends me to bed with a headache and tired, aching bones. She is my confessional and my comforter; I sometimes repeat to her words that were hurtfully exchanged in the daily gunfire of family life.

My mother always gives me good advice. She always puts a positive spin on things. She works miracles with my head.

The first time I realized my mother had these magic powers was when I was pregnant with Miranda. I was crying on the telephone, queasy with morning sickness, upset that I wasn't able to eat green vegetables as the doctor had recommended. "Why do you need to eat green veggies?" my mother innocently asked me.

"Because green veggies help develop brain cells, Mom!" I said, probably annoyed, thinking the world was about to end because my child was not getting the greenness she or he needed to grow well.

My mother simply said this: "Listen, I had three children—*three*—and I didn't eat green vegetables when I was pregnant. And all of your brains turned out lovely."

Only a mother could say that with a straight face and mean it. I laughed, realized how ridiculous this "newfangled motherhood" sometimes was, and decided then and there to relax and just be as healthy as possible during my pregnancy.

Then ten years later, when I didn't think our international adoption would happen, when things looked bleak in Guatemala, when hope was starting to fade, my mother told me to believe. She was right. Against amazing odds, Lucy became my daughter.

My mother loves life, and she loves me.

She lets me vent.

She listens to me when there is nothing to say.

She believes in me and is proud of my accomplishments.

And, most importantly, my mother guides me as a mother, nurturing my mothering skills and providing me with much-needed wisdom and sympathy. Degree or no degree, she is without a doubt the smartest person I know. ❁

Her children rise up and call her blessed.

PROVERBS 31:28A

Smarty Pants

Katherine Ellison, author of *The Mommy Brain: How Motherhood Makes Us Smarter*, claims that becoming a mom may make you more perceptive and observant, as well as heighten your motivation and ability to multitask. Plus, some new research indicates that oxytocin, the hormone involved with pregnancy and breastfeeding, may improve a mom's capacity for learning and memory.

It's a matter of survival, really: Having kids requires a cat's reflexes and an elephant's memory, not to mention the ability to discern the red sweater at the bottom of the laundry pile. Being a mom is a little like being a superhero. But you've known that all along. ✾

Who in their infinite wisdom decreed that Little League uniforms be white? Certainly not a mother.

ERMA BOMBECK

AN OUNCE OF MOTHER IS
WORTH A POUND OF PRIESTS.

SPANISH PROVERB

The Walking Stick

ELECE HOLLIS

I ran around to the back of the house. Mama, who had been peacefully pinning little shirts and dresses onto the clothesline, came running. We collided as I rounded the corner. The breath knocked out of me, I couldn't possibly answer her question: "Why is he screaming?" She raked me aside and ran on.

Our house was a split level with the basement exposed at the back. The hill sloped down toward the river that curved below like a snake in its bed. Our favorite tree resided on the edge of that slope, and its roots on the lower side, like the basement of the house, were exposed.

My little brother, Kent, and I had been happily playing in the sand at its base, digging, pouring, and shoveling to our heart's content, when Kent had suddenly erupted with a violent screams. This was no ordinary screaming. It was at the volume and pitch of raw terror. Instinctively, I ran.

I followed Mama back around the house then to the spot where Kent stood frozen with fear. His eyes were wide as saucers and he pointed to the ground at his feet.

I imagined a huge, coiled rattlesnake about to strike. I suppose Mama had the same thought. She attempted to snatch Kent up to whisk him away from the sand.

"Mama," he shrieked, "Look at it! It's an alive stick! I tried to pick it up to poke the sand and it moved! It walked! It has legs!"

Mama turned back to the tree to look. Kent scrambled down to study the stick more closely, his fear overcome by curiosity. We watched amazed as the slender brown twig pushed itself forward across the sand. Its six tiny legs moved again and it climbed over the handle of my sand shovel, stopping to fold its legs and hide itself. Kent poked at it and away it went.

Mama laughed with relief and sat down under the tree with us. She explained all she knew about the insect. She pointed out how wise and wonderful God was to create animals, birds, and insects with natural camouflage protection. The walking stick could lay still and become a twig, and a bird out searching for dinner would pass him by.

Mama talked about owls with feathers speckled brown and white to blend in with the bark of trees, and about arctic foxes and polar bears as white as snow. She told us about lizards and grasshoppers costumed in the green of grass and fish that looked like rocks on the ocean floor.

Kent spent the next hour following that walking stick around, and the remainder of the summer hunting for more. And when he was grown, he joined an entomology club.

My mother was a genius. In a moment when I had panicked, completely unsure of what to do, she had stepped in and saved the day. She turned a little boy's fear of the unknown into inspiration and in her God-given wisdom made curiosity a way of life.

She gave my brother and me a gift that day—a gift that has lived on. I have tried to follow her example of teaching and guiding as I parent my own kids. I've kept my head in moments of panic and walked alongside my children through unfamiliar situations. My mother might have thought she was merely passing along her knowledge of the animal kingdom. But she really passed along her wisdom for life. ❁

My son, keep your father's commands,
and don't forget your mother's teaching.

PROVERBS 6:20 NCV

God's Promises
for Finding Wisdom

For the Lord gives wisdom;
From His mouth come knowledge and understanding.

PROVERBS 2:6

Happy is the person who finds wisdom,
the one who gets understanding.

PROVERBS 3:13 NCV

Observe and obey all these words which I command you,
that it may go well with you and your children
after you forever, when you do what is good
and right in the sight of the Lord your God.

DEUTERONOMY 12:28

Train up a child in the way he should go,
And when he is old he will not depart from it.

PROVERBS 22:6

*The Sovereign Lord is
my strength; he makes my feet
like the feet of a deer, he
enables me to go on the heights.*

HABAKKUK 3:19A NIV

THE GIFT OF STRENGTH

There's nothing like motherhood to introduce us to our need for strength—strength to get up at 2 A.M. *again*, strength to withstand a grocery-store tantrum, strength to hang in there when our child is hurt or struggling.

When we commit our parenting to the Lord, He offers us His strength in abundance. His resources can never be depleted; His office is never closed. Whatever the situation, He infuses us with His strength, and we are able to pass it on to our children.

YOU CAN LEARN MANY
THINGS FROM CHILDREN.
HOW MUCH PATIENCE
YOU HAVE, FOR INSTANCE.

FRANKLIN P. JONES

Clothes Closet Capers

PATRICIA LORENZ

Mothers and teenage daughters know what it's like. Shopping for clothes together at the local mall is a test of patience, physical endurance, restraint, and basic human kindness. I remember many trips to the mall with my two daughters.

"Mother, give it up! These pants are way too baggy!"

"Honey, they're skin tight. They'd split if you sat down! And after they've been in the dryer, why—"

"Mom, you're so old fashioned!"

Later, in the shoe store, the sharp-edged conversation would begin again. "Well, Mom, these shoes are alright, I guess. They look just like the name-brand ones and they fit okay, but Mother, they don't have the right label. And that's why they're not cool. Everybody will know I got them at a discount store! I'll pay the twenty-dollar difference myself for the name-brand ones, okay?"

"When donkeys fly, you will. If you have that kind of money to throw around, you can put it in your college fund."

We move on to the fancy dress store. "No, I don't like that dress. It's straight out of the eighties! Do you actually think I'd be caught dead in a dress like that?"

"No, I was thinking more in terms of the homecoming dance, but if you keep talking to me like this . . ."

Please, Lord, give me patience. Direct me out of this store and over to the place where they sell warm chocolate chip cookies. Quickly, Lord.

By the time they were in high school I'd had about all the dismal, distressing, argumentative shopping trips I could stand. I decided to let them shop alone from then on with money they earned themselves.

Thanks, Lord, for that brilliant idea. Maybe I'll survive motherhood after all.

Then one day, a year or so later, it happened.

"Mom," Julia asked sweetly, "may I borrow your yellow blouse to wear to school tomorrow? And maybe your blue and yellow print skirt?"

"Sure, honey!" I practically fell off the stool at the kitchen counter. At last my daughters were growing up. Our taste in clothes was starting to meld. I suddenly felt ten years younger.

A few minutes later, Jeanne passed through the kitchen.

"Mom, could I try on some of your clothes? I might like to borrow your plaid skirt and one of your scarves."

"Help yourself, my dear," I smiled smugly as I turned up the music on their favorite radio station. *I love having daughters,* I thought to myself.

Oh, Lord, thank You. Either I'm getting really hip when it comes to clothes, or they've finally discovered sensible fashion. Whatever it is, Lord, let me cherish this moment.

Suddenly, being a single mom was fun. Instead of fighting over the cost of clothes and the styles my daughters wanted versus those that actually made sense to me, visions of exciting mother-daughter shopping sprees danced in my head. Why, now we could plan whole days of shopping, I mused. We could look at stores and magazines, share ideas about fashion, and help each other choose styles that flattered us.

I continued to dream. There would be lunches, quiche and croissants, iced tea, and maybe we three would split a dessert, all the while discussing our bargains and look-alike fashions. The dream was filling my heart with the joy of motherhood.

Just then Jeanne and Julia emerged from my bedroom dressed practically head to toe in fashions from my wardrobe, including jewelry and other accessories.

"Thanks, Mom! Your clothes are great!" they bubbled.

I wasn't so sure about the combinations they'd chosen, but I certainly wasn't about to criticize. After all, I didn't want to ruin this special moment, this tender passage from teendom to a more sophisticated world of young women.

"Yeah, they're perfect, Mom," Jeanne nodded. "It's nerd day at school tomorrow—you know, everybody dresses up like the fifties, real dorky-like. These things are perfect!"

"Oh . . ."

Lord, are You there? I need more patience, Lord. Lots more. Right this minute, Lord. Are You listening? ❀

> *Smart people are patient; they will*
> *be honored if they ignore insults.*
>
> PROVERBS 19:11 NCV

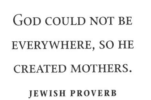

GOD COULD NOT BE
EVERYWHERE, SO HE
CREATED MOTHERS.

JEWISH PROVERB

Energy Boost

If the long days are starting to get to you, try these fatigue fighters—

- **Exercise.** Cramming a workout into an already full mom schedule is easier said than done, of course, but exercise can work wonders to keep you mentally and physically on your toes.
- **Drink water.** Plenty of water helps your brain and body run on all four cylinders. Conventional wisdom tells us to drink eight eight-ounce glasses of water a day. As a rule, don't wait until you're thirsty to reach for a glass of water.
- **Eat breakfast.** It really is the most important meal of the day—breakfast gives your body a good start to the day and helps keep your energy level up. Take it easy on the sugar at the breakfast table, and try to include a balance of protein and carbohydrates.

- **Think protein.** Protein is your friend throughout the day. It affects your body's absorption of other energy-bearing nutrients and is tied to the brain chemicals that have to do with alertness, acuity, and attention.

Take care of yourself. You may be Supermom, but everyone needs to replenish their energy stores now and then. Take a minute to rest and thank God for His amazing energy and strength. ❀

ANY MOTHER COULD PERFORM THE JOBS OF
SEVERAL AIR TRAFFIC CONTROLLERS WITH EASE.

LISA ALTHER

SNUGGLE IN GOD'S ARMS.
WHEN YOU ARE HURTING,
WHEN YOU FEEL LONELY, LEFT
OUT, LET HIM CRADLE YOU,
COMFORT YOU, REASSURE
YOU OF HIS ALL-SUFFICIENT
POWER AND LOVE.

KAY ARTHUR

A Thankful Heart

NANETTE THORSEN-SNIPES

That fall day was supposed to be a day set aside for giving thanks—Thanksgiving. But as the wind whistled outside my kitchen window on that dreary afternoon, I was feeling less than thankful. I fished another boiled egg from the large pan. I began shelling, and I could feel the heat of anger rush to my cheeks. My husband had helped me start the small turkey, then squirreled himself away on the sofa.

"Do you need any help?" he asked as he peered from behind the sports page.

"No," I answered tersely. I tossed the half-peeled egg into the pan. I could feel the tears building, and I fought the feelings of self-pity. I picked up the hospital bracelet my daughter had just removed and threw it in the trash.

Just two days earlier, I had rushed my teenaged daughter, Jamie, to the emergency room. For nine long hours, I stood beside her wondering what caused the severe pains in her stomach. The emergency room doctor poked, prodded, and tested my daughter as she continued to double over in pain, often retching into a plastic pan.

One by one, the doctor ruled out ulcers, kidney problems, stomach virus, pelvic infection. . . . About midday, I felt relieved to see our family doctor. He gingerly felt her abdomen causing her to shrink from his hand. I noticed he kept coming back to her right side, watching her reaction. Finally, he stepped back and said he thought it was her appendix.

By 9:00 that evening, Jamie had her inflamed appendix removed. While her problem had disappeared on the operating table, mine had just begun.

I had hoped the bustling activities of the Thanksgiving holiday at my son's house would keep me busy. In fact, I'd hoped I would be so busy I wouldn't remember that Thanksgiving was the time of year my former husband, my boys' father, chose to commit suicide. But now, with my daughter's surgery still fresh, Jamie would be unable to make the trip to my son's. And the memory would linger at the edge of my mind.

I stood at the kitchen sink, my head pounding. A lone tear trailed my face. I dialed my next-door neighbor and friend, Donna. "Do you have any aspirin?" I asked, trying to keep my voice from quivering.

"No, but I'll be glad to pick some up for you," she said cheerily, indicating she had to go out anyway.

I sighed. "That's all right. I really need to get out."
My voice cracked as I added, "This is just not a good day
for me." I hung up the phone. Nothing had gone right.
Thanksgiving? What a joke. I was incapable of being
thankful for anything.

I drove alone to the store, my nose still red from
crying. I felt so exhausted, so tired. I wondered how I
would ever make this small Thanksgiving come together
for my husband and two teenaged kids.

Deep down, I knew I should pray, but I was so
wrapped up in my self-pity, I really didn't have the energy.
By the time I drove back to my house I felt weak, and I just
wanted to crawl into bed.

As I pulled into the carport, I noticed a little pot of gaily-
wrapped lavender flowers beside my back door. *Jamie is so
well loved*, I thought gratefully. My daughter's friends had
shown up all week with flowers, teddy bears, and videos. I
brought the flowers inside and set them on my table.

To my surprise, the simple white piece of paper
in the flowerpot had my name on it. "His strength is
perfect when our strength is gone," it read. As I turned
the paper over I realized it was from Donna, who was
busy with a large family gathering next door. The

heaviness in my heart began to lift. I knew in my heart that she was right.

I touched the soft lavender petals thinking how thoughtless I'd been. Right there, I bowed my head and whispered a prayer. "Thank You for a neighbor like Donna who cares enough to give me flowers for my broken heart."

Sometimes when we can't get beyond our own self-pity, God in His infinite wisdom provides a neighborly act of kindness to get us back on the right path.

When I returned to my pan of eggs, my husband stood by my side, shelling an egg. The smell of the roasting turkey filled the room. He placed his arm around me and kissed my cheek, and my heart overflowed with thanks. ❧

*He gives strength
to those who are tired
and more power
to those who are weak.*

Isaiah 40:29 NCV

MANY PEOPLE WILL
WALK IN AND OUT OF
YOUR LIFE, BUT ONLY TRUE
FRIENDS WILL LEAVE
FOOTPRINTS IN YOUR HEART.

ELEANOR ROOSEVELT

A Knowing Friend

LOUISE TUCKER JONES

A sigh of relief escaped me as the morning worship service ended and parents began to pick up their toddlers. Normally, I enjoyed helping out in the nursery every other Sunday, but today a new member was helping me. She was the mother of one of the toddlers, as was I. But our boys were opposites. My Aaron was quiet, calm, and a little bigger than the other children. Her David was small, wiry, and hyper.

Throughout the hour, she never seemed to notice as he flew airplanes across the room, jumped on and off chairs, and zipped around the room with his built-in sirens going at full blast.

Phyllis was pregnant, laughed a lot, and seemed to enjoy everybody and everything. Though I liked her, I couldn't relax in the midst of such confusion.

I left the nursery that morning with no intention of ever working with this woman again. Little did I know that she would become my best friend—and that she would love and help me through a tragedy.

Being members of a small church, Phyllis and I saw

each other every Sunday and Wednesday. We soon learned that we lived only blocks apart. Though I knew I should be sociable, I just couldn't imagine our boys getting along with each other. But Phyllis never gave that a thought. She went right on building our new friendship and didn't seem to notice my reluctance to accept an invitation to her home for dinner—the kind of invitation I knew I should have extended first.

And so, feeling a little guilty, I went with my husband to dine with Phyllis and her husband, Neil, later that week. To my surprise, Aaron and David got along famously. After that we visited often in each other's homes. And before long, we had become best friends.

There was only one part of our friendship that made me uncomfortable. Whenever Phyllis talked about Jeff, their son who had died right before David was born, I looked at the ground and struggled to find words. I just didn't know how to respond to such a tragedy. Yet Phyllis was full of joy and love, not bitterness or anger. Though I couldn't understand it, she exhibited genuine peace.

Soon Phyllis gave birth to Jenny and we marveled at all her newness. Several months later our second son, Travis, was born. Everyone shared our happiness, especially Phyllis and Neil.

But then without warning, our secure, happy world fell apart. I called Phyllis from the hospital emergency room.

"It's Travis," I said, my voice and body shaking with fear. "They don't know if he will make it."

"We'll be right there," she said quickly. And they were.

Travis died about eight hours later. It was a rare congenital heart condition, something the doctors had failed to diagnose at birth. It was sudden, shocking, and the most painful thing I have ever experienced. Family and friends hovered over me, doing everything they could to help, but Phyllis really knew how I felt. She encouraged me to talk and even expressed my feelings for me on occasion.

"You feel a great big hole in your heart," Phyllis said, "and there is nothing to fill it up."

Oh, how right she was. I had never felt such emptiness, such pain. But Phyllis had traveled this road before me and comforted me in the following days, weeks, and months with words, tears, hugs and even laughter. On a card she wrote, "Now heaven is sweeter because Travis is there." God had not left me alone; He had sent me a friend who understood exactly how my world was breaking down.

A year later my husband accepted a job transfer to another city. I knew absolutely no one and deeply missed

Phyllis and her sunny disposition. Since we were only an hour and half apart, we continued to visit, celebrating the birth of her son, Mark, and the adoption of our daughter, Paula. But by the time I gave birth to our son, Jay, with Down syndrome, Phyllis had moved to another state, ten hours away.

Despite the distance, cards, calls, and sporadic visits continued. One day I might answer the phone and unexpectedly hear a familiar chuckle on the end of the line followed by, "Hi, Lou!" Time would slip away and it was like we were young mothers again, living only blocks apart instead of being separated by a couple of states.

Years passed, but our friendship remained strong. And then I received a late-night call from Jenny, Phyllis's now grown daughter. Her mother had lost her battle with cancer. My heart wrenched with pain at the loss of my longtime friend, yet I had to smile as Jenny told me how her mother laughed and talked throughout the last night of her life at the hospital. She even heard angels singing. It was so like her.

And heaven is sweeter because Phyllis is there. ❦

My God will use his wonderful riches in
Christ Jesus to give you everything you need.

PHILIPPIANS 4:19 NCV

God's Promises for Strength

It is God who arms me with strength,
And makes my way perfect.

PSALM 18:32

He gives strength to those who are tired
and more power to those who are weak.

ISAIAH 40:29 NCV

He restores my soul; He leads me in the
paths of righteousness For His name's sake.

PSALM 23:3

Come to Me, all you who labor and are heavy laden,
and I will give you rest. Take My yoke upon you and
learn from Me, for I am gentle and lowly in heart,
and you will find rest for your souls. For My yoke
is easy and My burden is light.

MATTHEW 11:28–30

You will keep him in perfect peace,
Whose mind is stayed on You,
Because he trusts in You.

ISAIAH 26:3

THE GIFT
OF PEACE
WHEN THERE
ARE TRIALS

―――――――――

"Into every life a little rain must fall." So goes the old saying. We all experience tough days, challenging days— and days when we feel our hearts are breaking.

In the midst of our darkest days, our heavenly Father comes beside us, offering us a place of refuge and shelter. He gives us His peace and enables us to stand strong on behalf of our family. When we trust in Him, the rains that come our way need not wash away our joy and resolve.

TO ME, EVERY HOUR
OF THE DAY AND NIGHT
IS AN UNSPEAKABLY
PERFECT MIRACLE.

WALT WHITMAN

A Daily Dose of Miracles

LOUISE TUCKER JONES

Having already experienced the death of my middle son due to a rare congenital heart defect, I was devastated to learn that my beautiful newborn baby boy not only had Down syndrome but congenital heart disease as well.

"It's not the same thing that Travis had," my doctor assured me. "It's a hole between the chambers—probably a small one, and it may even close on its own."

But at fifteen months old, the hole in Jay's heart had not closed, and it was decided that open heart surgery was the best course of action. A heart catheterization—a minor surgical procedure—would be done beforehand to determine the extent of the problem and make sure the surgeon met no surprises on the operating table.

On the morning of the cath, I held Jay's sleepy, sedated body in my arms as long as possible, then walked beside him as they wheeled him down the hall on what seemed like a giant-sized gurney.

After about an hour or so, my husband and I were ushered into the cath lab, X-rays glowing large on two full walls. Jay lay on the cath table, still sedated and nearly as white as the sheets that surrounded him. A nipple stuffed with cotton was taped to his mouth, where a nurse had dripped sugar water to pacify him. It shook me to see him so still and pale. I wanted to pick him up and run home, but the doctor claimed my attention.

"I called you in here because I wanted you to see what we found. It's not good." And all of a sudden, I'd walked into my worst-case scenario. The doctor explained that Jay had already developed pulmonary hypertension, a condition that made open heart surgery so risky that the physician advised against it.

"I don't believe he would ever come off the heart-lung machine if we went through with the surgery," he said, apologizing for such devastating news. He had never known of a child so young to develop pulmonary hypertension. It surprised everyone.

Without the surgery, Jay's life expectancy would probably be short. If he managed to avoid any major respiratory infections like pneumonia, he might live into early adolescence. I was in total shock. Was this a choice? Were they asking us if we wanted Jay to die now or die later? I was so tired, confused, and frightened that I couldn't even cry.

We followed the gurney to Jay's room where we waited the next eight hours while he was monitored on a regular basis. I picked him up and rocked him, just wanting to hold him and protect him. I looked into his sweet, sleeping face, still pale and lifeless, and knew I could never send him into surgery where the odds were greater that he would die than survive. We would take the years we had with him, even if they were few.

But my prayer was that God would perform a miracle in Jay's life and heal his heart disease. The Down syndrome was no big deal to us, but I had learned from experience that heart disease is deadly.

Within a few years, Jay had managed to astound just about everyone, especially the medical community, with his energy and vivacious personality even as the heart disease progressed. Upper respiratory infections were rampant during the winter, and he had several bouts with pneumonia. Still, he survived. But he didn't just survive. Jay celebrated life. He would sing and dance to music, chase the waves at the beach, play T-ball with friends, and aggravate his brother and sister.

By his teen years Jay's skin began taking on a slightly dusky appearance and he began to tire more easily.

Doctors warned us of impending strokes or a fatal cardiac arrhythmia, but I continued to pray for a miracle. I wanted to walk into that cardiologist's office one day and hear him say, "Why, Mrs. Jones, we have no idea what has happened, but Jay's tests show that there is absolutely no heart disease present." That's what I prayed for—a real live miracle. But it didn't happen.

Soon Jay began to sleep with oxygen at night—but he still danced to his music during the daytime, dazzled friends at church every Sunday with his suit and tie, and often went bowling or rented favorite videos. He was a joy to be around, smiling and laughing, hugging and loving everyone he met.

After an extremely serious episode of pneumonia that landed Jay in the hospital for a week, we began schooling him at home to cut down on upper respiratory infections. We still gave him social interaction with other people, but we were extremely careful, making sure he wasn't around anyone who was sick with a cold, the flu, or a virus, and we did more than our share of hand washing. Friends and family knew not to visit if they were not well. It became a way of life, but I kept praying for a miracle, and Jay continued to dance to his music and go out for his daily Coke.

When Jay turned twenty, we had a grand celebration, calling it his "miracle birthday." He had far exceeded all the doctors' expectations. Not too long after, I visited briefly with his longtime cardiologist and said, "Tell me the truth. You never expected to ever see this day, did you?" He conceded that he did not. Perhaps none of us really thought we would ever see that day—none of us except Jay.

Jay never worries about tomorrow. He lives every day in the present, squeezing all of the life he can from it and then spreading it like sunshine to everyone around him. I feel blessed just being his mother. And somewhere along the way, in his now thirty years, I found that I had stopped praying for a miracle and began thanking God for the one I had. It wasn't the miraculous healing I'd prayed for those many years ago, but I finally realized that we had indeed received our very own miracle. We just got it in daily doses. ❦

The eyes of the Lord are on the righteous,
And His ears are open to their cry.

PSALM 34:15 NKJV

From "Love Speaks"

BY IDA M. FOLSOM

If I could stand, dear child of mine,
Between the world and you,
And keep your life untouched by sin,
The sordid from your view;

If I could make the world come close,
Yet yield but precious truths,
And keeping back the pain of life,
Give only that which soothes . . .

There is a pain that purifies;
Loss may be gain, I know;
Each life must bear its own proud load,
And reap what it shall sow.

But standing by each hour, my child,
My heart shall bleed anew,
For every pain that comes to you
Shall be to me as two!

He takes care of his people like a shepherd. He gathers them like lambs in his arms and carries them close to him. He gently leads the mothers of the lambs.

ISAIAH 40:11 NCV

TRUST THE PAST TO
GOD'S MERCY, THE PRESENT
TO GOD'S LOVE AND THE FUTURE
TO GOD'S PROVIDENCE.

AUGUSTINE

My Prodigal Son

NANETTE THORSEN-SNIPES

The feeling of terror creeps back into my life. This time it is my son, not my former husband. However, the same elements are in place—the gun, the ever-present fear, the rage. I sit at my kitchen table and stare at the shards of light dancing in my coffee cup. The coffee is cold now. And the night wears on my nerves as I wait for my son to come home.

I cup my hands around the mug painted brightly with yellow daisies. When he was little, my son gave it to me for my birthday. He was always bringing me flowers. Usually, they were tightly clasped in his small, sweaty fist. With a toothless grin, he would say, "These are for you, Mama." I would kneel down at eye level with him and hug him. Then I would take the wilting wildflowers from his hand and place them in a jelly jar on my kitchen table.

I pour the cold coffee into the sink. My heart seems to be breaking as I remember the last few months. My teenager's anger erupted over the least thing.

"This bike is no good," I remember him screaming as he slammed the ten-speed again and again into the ground until it lay in a crumpled heap. He had used the money he worked so hard for to buy the bike. But for some reason it wouldn't work properly, and he became angry.

I cringed at his foul language. And I feared his hostility. One day in an angry rage, he rammed his fist through the door leading to the basement and he shattered the mirror in his bedroom. His drinking was becoming a problem too, but I didn't know how to stop him.

The anger was so terribly familiar. His father had had the same anger. It seethed for years under a cool exterior until he finally exploded and threatened my life with a loaded gun. My former husband's life had ended abruptly. Now my son had stolen a gun from our bedroom closet, and the same anger boiled inside him.

I watched Jim, my husband, pace the living room floor. His brow furrowed in worry. "Where is he?" he asked.

I shrugged and glanced at the digital clock on the television. I too was exhausted from worrying. "It's 1:00 and we still haven't heard from him," I said.

My exhausted mind continued to run, reflecting on the situation at hand. Many times I'd heard the phrase "Let go and let God." For months, I had been worrying about how to handle Donnie. Maybe it was time to turn my wandering son over to the Lord. This time I knew I had to leave my child in God's hands instead of taking him back.

I sat down at the kitchen table, bowed my head, and prayed. And in that one moment I felt a complete peace wash over me as I turned my son over to the Lord.

"I'm just putting him totally and completely in God's hands," I told my husband quietly. I crawled into bed knowing God was in control. Later, I felt my husband slip into bed.

At 1:30 A.M., the ringing phone jarred us awake. Sleepily, I answered. The police officer on the other end informed me that once again my teenager had broken the law and was in jail. This time he had started a fight with a bouncer in a hotel lounge. When the security people found the gun on him, they called in seven or eight police cars. I was relieved to learn the gun was unloaded, but it didn't make the charges any less serious.

"I have been praying about this," my husband said after I hung up, "and I feel a real peace about what I'm about to say. I don't think we should bail him out of jail again."

A lump stuck in my throat. I swallowed over it. I knew, after all the times my son had been jailed for drunk driving, that my husband was right. But it was hard to turn away from my own flesh and blood. I feared losing him forever.

When my son called the next morning asking us to put up bail, my husband simply said, "We are through bailing you out of jail. This time you'll have to get out on your own." My husband sighed as he hung up. "He's mad," he said.

I'd often wondered how a parent could not come to a child's rescue. I had to learn the hard way that if I continued to get my child out of trouble, he would never take any responsibility for his own actions. And he would continue to get himself into trouble.

A few days later my son came home. He didn't speak to either of us except to say, "I'm moving out." He and a friend loaded his car with my son's belongings and left.

Several months went by before I heard from him again. He drove up the driveway one day, and I saw a blonde-haired girl by his side. He was smiling as he and the young woman walked into the house. The four of us sat down in the living room and talked. I was delighted to learn he wanted to get married. Although I had some well-founded apprehensions about his past anger, I certainly hoped he and his future wife would be happy.

As the days, weeks, and months flew by, I began to see a profound change in my married son. The angry young man who left our home seemed to melt away as he became involved with his new family. And eventually, to my great happiness, he turned his life over to God.

At one of our first Christmases together after his marriage, my son drove to the store with my husband. The cab of the truck was almost silent except for the radio playing softly. My son broke the quiet with an unexpected question. "Can you ever forgive me for the pain I put you through?" he asked.

My husband smiled, put his arm around him and said, "I've been waiting for you to come home, Donnie—really come home. I've already forgiven you."

I thank the Lord for bringing my wandering son home. And I thank my husband for having a forgiving spirit and welcoming my son home with compassion, just as the father of the biblical prodigal son did.

My son still brings me flowers. That same Christmas, he brought a gorgeous poinsettia and set it on my kitchen table. Just as he did as a small child, he said, "These are for you, Mama." ✽

I waited patiently for the Lord;
And He inclined to me, And heard my cry.

PSALM 40:1B

Cry Out

When we're in the midst of trial, it's tempting to rush back into our routines before we've taken the time to lay our burden before our God. Whatever you're facing today, find a minute to cry out to the One who bears our burdens. Grab a journal and find a few Psalms (Psalms 4, 16, and 38 are particularly good) and simply pour your heart out before the Father who cares for you. And when you experience His sustaining peace and loving care, take time to cry out with thanksgiving and praise as well. ❦

O Lord, do not forsake me;
be not far from me, O my God.
Come quickly to help me,
O Lord my Savior.

PSALM 38:21–22 NIV

God's Promises for Enduring Trials

*Yea, though I walk through the valley of the shadow
of death, I will fear no evil; For You are with me;
Your rod and Your staff, they comfort me.*

PSALM 23:4

*Return to your fortress, O prisoners of hope; even now
I announce that I will restore twice as much to you.*

ZECHARIAH 9:12 NIV

*He heals the brokenhearted
And binds up their wounds.*

PSALM 147:3

*He comforts us in all our troubles so that we can comfort
others. When others are troubled, we will be able to give
them the same comfort God has given us.*

2 CORINTHIANS 1:4 NLT

*"For I know the plans
I have for you," says the* LORD.
*"They are plans for good and
not for disaster, to give you
a future and a hope."*

JEREMIAH 29:11 NLT

THE GIFT OF LETTING GO AT THE RIGHT TIME

Who knew it would all happen so quickly? One moment you're driving home from the hospital, and the next you're driving your child to kindergarten—and then to college.

None of this would be so bad, except that as our kids grow a little more independent every day, they need us a little less every day, and our relationship changes. Plus, doing what's best for them sometimes means turning off our natural protective instinct, no easy task for any mother. Put simply, letting go is challenging.

We can take comfort in knowing that when we let go, we're not simply thrusting our kids off into the void; we're committing them into the hands of a capable Father. And that same Father enables us to meet all the challenges of motherhood.

EVERY EVENING I TURN
MY TROUBLES OVER TO GOD—
HE'S GOING TO BE UP
ALL NIGHT ANYWAY.

DONALD J. MORGAN

Put Your Worry Alarm on Snooze

MARGARET LANG

My daughter, Karin, was on a plane, embarking on her first missionary journey to a distant land. I had talked her into it, maybe not directly, but over years of sharing my experiences of serving people overseas in my youth. It was my hope that one of my two children would pick up the torch again.

And now that she had, I half wished she hadn't.

Wasn't she sort of young for this, still only in her teens? I waited for the phone to ring at the designated time of her arrival in South America. But no call came. My worry alarm started to beep. All alone. Foreign land. No language skills.

Bedtime came and went. I customarily slept in the guest room, which provided a more comfortable bed. But there was no phone in there. I pulled the phone cord as far down the hallway as it would reach and lay down on my great-grandparents' Victorian bedstead. In the mid-nineteenth century by horse-drawn wagon, they had pioneered a new life in the Rocky Mountains of the Wild West.

Now Karin was pioneering in the Andes. Would she make her way safely up the mountains and find the doctor she was supposed to observe treating the Indians?

I tucked the covers under my chin and recalled when Karin, my first child, was born. Her birth had startled me. A non-believer at the time, I had inquired loudly of the whole delivery room staff, "Where did she come from?" They looked at me like I was crazy. But I was amazed that such a beautifully formed human being had appeared seemingly out of nowhere. I knew then that there had to be a Designer and a design for her life.

Karin revealed her servant's heart with her first complete sentence: "Mommy, how can I help you?" No matter how difficult the circumstances in our single-mom family, she lent a hand around our farm.

If the goat needed milking, she milked it. If a possum died, she buried it. If wood needed to be carried to our stove, she carried it. If floors needed to be scrubbed, she scrubbed them; the barn swept, she swept it.

She often heard stories about her father, a doctor, and me riding horseback and crossing flooded streams to teach public health workers in mountainous Africa. She read about her great-grandfather, also a doctor, traveling by mule-drawn cart to deliver babies and treat the sick in West China.

Forging new territory is in her blood. But will that help her? I worried. I had heard talk about how parents sometimes needed to let go. I was growing surer and surer that this was one of those times, but I wasn't quite sure how to do it.

Tired of wrestling with my bedding and my fears, I finally turned to God. *You're omnipotent and You know exactly where she is. Please take the night watch. I need some sleep.* And I rolled over and dozed off.

When the morning light peeked through my window, I felt there was some great weight that had been temporarily set aside the night before, but I wasn't awake enough to remember what it was. Until the phone rang—and I took the burden back on my shoulders.

"Hello," I said with urgency and concern. Nothing but static. "Hello," I repeated more loudly.

Then heard a distant voice with a faint echo: "Mom, it's me . . . it's me. I'm safe in Bolivia . . . Bolivia."

"Thank God," I said.

"I am so sorry I couldn't call sooner." She waited for the echo to finish. "But the phone lines were all tied up."

I breathed a sigh of relief, one of many sighs to come in the years ahead.

Karin went to college and medical school and fulfilled her destiny to be a doctor and a missionary. Every time she went to an impoverished country, she warned me, "Put your worry alarm on snooze, Mom, because you know I always call right after your worry alarm goes off."

"Yes, dear, I'll try," I said. And I did try, and I got better. Yet even when she was thirty-five years old and off to the Himalayas, I still got a tinge of tightness in my heart until I heard her voice or read her e-mail—"Hi, Mom. I arrived safely."

Because I'm a missionary mom, somehow I believe God cuts me some slack. He knows my frame: dust. He knows how hard I try to let go and let God, and sometimes I actually succeed—well, almost.

Then He just gives me more rope and another try. What a patient and faithful God He is. ❀

For He knows our frame;
He remembers that we are dust.

PSALM 103:14 NKJV

THERE IS ONE THING
THAT GIVES RADIANCE
TO EVERYTHING. IT IS THE
IDEA OF SOMETHING
AROUND THE CORNER.

G. K. CHESTERTON

School Days

NANCY B. GIBBS

When my twin sons started kindergarten, I followed in my mother's footsteps by singing the song "School Days" while we were getting ready to go. I don't know if I sang it to make the boys laugh or if I was singing to cope with the fact that my boys didn't need me as much as they once had. I knew one thing for sure, however: The more I sang, the less likely I would cry.

That year sped by and the first day of the first grade was quickly upon us. Again, the air that morning was filled with my somewhat off-key rendition of "School Days."

"Oh, Mama," the boys groaned while fighting back the smiles, and that simple song turned another bittersweet day into a joyous occasion for me.

Every year on the first day of school, the scene was the same, from second grade, third, fourth, fifth, all the way up to the twelfth grade. I didn't care whether they liked it or not. The more they opposed, the louder I sang. Each year the song was a little easier to sing as I was learning to accept the fact that my sons were getting older.

But on the morning of their last year of high school, tears filled my eyes as I sang. I knew that the next year would be quite different. I probably wouldn't see them their first morning of college classes, since there were no colleges in our immediate area. Even though I had prepared myself for my sons to grow up, I wasn't ready for them to leave home. Not just yet.

The night before their first day of classes at their new college, Chad called home. He was so excited and wanted to share with us all about his books and the professors that he had met (along with a few girls, he hinted). Before we hung up, Chad asked, "My first class starts at 8:00 tomorrow, Mama. Are you going to call me? We have to leave at 7:30."

"Do you want me to call, son?" I asked.

"Yes, Mama, I do," Chad said. "You have to sing 'School Days.'"

"What if I just go ahead and sing it tonight?" I asked.

"But Mama, it just won't be the same," Chad declared.

At 7:00 sharp the next morning, I called, singing to both boys. They were both laughing when we hung up our phones.

I smiled as I started my day, knowing that God had just given me a wonderful blessing. True, the season of my life with my sons at home was over. But a new season of fond memories of happy days had just begun. ❧

With the loving mercy of our God,
a new day from heaven will dawn upon us.

LUKE 1:78 NCV

Taking Responsibility

If your kids are younger, your letting-go duties may be smaller than if your kids are heading off to college. Nonetheless, no matter how old our kids are, we need to take steps to prepare them for success.

To strengthen your kids' responsibility muscles (and your letting-go muscles), give each of your kids an age-appropriate bonus responsibility this week. Help your school-age child pick a hobby, or have your high schooler help out with shuttling her siblings to practices and activities. You'll enjoy watching them grow just a little more independent, a little more confident—even if it means letting them go. ❀

THE LOVE OF A PARENT FOR A CHILD IS THE
LOVE THAT SHOULD GROW TOWARDS SEPARATION.

KAHLIL GIBRAN

THE GREATEST GIFTS
YOU CAN GIVE YOUR
CHILDREN ARE THE
ROOTS OF RESPONSIBILITY
AND THE WINGS
OF INDEPENDENCE.

DENIS WAITLEY

I Couldn't Let Go of My Children, So They Let Go of Me

JOAN CLAYTON

I suppose I thought it would last forever. What wonderful years we had—rock hunting, picnics, Little League, band, basketball, all the other fun things you do with your kids. Birthdays and holidays all centered on our sons.

Of course we had our share of anxious moments, like trips to the hospital in the middle of the night for croup and various daytime injuries usually incurred during baseball or football.

One accident in particular is emblazoned on my memory. Our two younger boys were playing blind man's bluff. Lane, the youngest, was blindfolded. He stumbled over a jagged rock, fell, and hit his head. A big knot appeared on his forehead and my husband, Emmitt, took him to the emergency room immediately. Fortunately, the wound wasn't serious, so the attendants treated Lane and then sent them home.

When I returned home from shopping, I found Mark, our oldest son, in tears. Lance, our middle son, apparently felt guilty about Lane's accident and had disappeared. Next to the front door was a note: "Dear Dad, I've run away. I cause too much trouble. Bye. Lance."

We searched and searched. We drove up and down our street and all around the neighborhood, but no Lance appeared.

Finally the family dog sniffed Lance out from his hiding place behind the butane tank. Relief flooded my heart as Emmitt swooped up Lance in his arms and showered him with kisses.

Many mornings we woke to find three lively boys in our bed. After the inevitable wrestling match, we would all end up on the floor in uncontrollable laughter.

When I caught them red-handed in the cookie jar, they tried to throw me off track by charming me. "Mommy, will you marry us when we grow up?" (It worked.) Amidst all our fun times together, I did not realize how quickly time was slipping away.

It only hit home the morning after Mark's wedding. I went into his room and opened his closet, and the shock of seeing the bare shelves triggered a sudden outburst of tears.

The closet was completely empty except for one tiny bowl containing his two front baby teeth, a cat's-eye marble, two round pebbles for skipping on water, and a little rusty chain. I collapsed on the bed. Was this really all there was, all I had left of my years with Mark? Where had the time gone?

I couldn't let him go, even though he was married. I guess I wanted—expected—our relationship to stay the same; he was still my little boy, in my eyes. But naturally, in the months following the wedding, we didn't see him as much, and in my self-pity, I interpreted this as rejection.

Everywhere I turned, I saw reminders of him. The white paint still lingered on the red brick wall where he and his brother had had a paint fight. The paint finally wore off the dog's fur, but it remained on the wall to remind me.

I felt Mark had deserted his family—after everything we had done for him. I didn't realize that he desperately needed his independence, the freedom to make his own decisions and be the man of his own household. I went around for months with my feelings on my shoulder, bandaged in a giant dose of "poor little me."

By the time our middle son married, I had turned into a real clinging vine, causing him to be almost psychologically dependent on my husband and me. How I thank God he had an understanding wife who helped him mature in spite of my clinging and interfering. After his college graduation, they moved a thousand miles away, and my heart ached until I thought it couldn't hurt anymore.

"I can't tell you goodbye!" I cried when he left.

"But, Mom," Lance replied, holding me with all the might of his six-foot-four frame, "a Christian never has to say goodbye."

By this time, our youngest son, Lane, was graduating from high school. I told him, "Lane, when you walk across that stage, I'm going to run up there, grab you, and say, 'That's my baby!'"

Lane knew I wouldn't dare, but he did something that graduation night that is forever sealed in my heart.

Emmitt, being the high-school principal, always announced each graduate's name and then shook his or her hand. Since he had always treated our boys like any other student while they were at school, he planned to simply shake Lane's hand after he called his name.

But when he announced, "Tony Lane Clayton," amid the applause and cheers of the other students, Lane walked right up to his daddy, embraced him with outstretched arms, and held him close. I burst into tears.

A minister came to me after the graduation ceremony. "You must have a wonderful family," he said. "It is very rare to see a boy show such affection to his parents in public." I cried again.

Two years later, I cried some more. Lane cried too. He had packed everything he owned into his car, ready to leave home.

"But why are you leaving?" I cried.

"You've been great parents, but it's time for me to grow up."

By now Lane had discovered through his brothers' experiences that his independence could only be achieved away from me.

Looking back, I can see that my own emotional insecurity had forced my children to flee the nest. Unlike the eagle who pushes her babies out of the nest, I would have clung to them until the nest disintegrated.

Letting go is still hard for me, even now with six grandchildren. After a visit, it takes about a week to get over seeing them. I don't know which is worse, not seeing them often enough, or telling them goodbye when they go back home. Maybe this is psychological dependence on my part. Or maybe it's wishing the time had not passed so quickly.

I have the same feeling every May when I tell my second graders goodbye at school. I think, *Why didn't I love them more and teach them less?*

The boys are happy leading their own lives and I'm thankful. Sure, they make mistakes. When they first started to walk, we didn't stop them, even though we knew they would fall sometimes. The same is true when they leave the nest. They are going to fall sometimes. How else can they learn? It goes against nature to try to keep them from developing. But by not letting go, I was stunting their growth. Can you imagine a mother cat carrying her baby kittens around by the nape of the neck their entire lives?

As a dear friend said to me one day, "In order to keep them, you have to let them go."

I have finally learned to put my children in God's hands and trust Him. He loves them even more than I do. My role has now changed from that of being a parent to being a strong supporter and friend.

Plus, I have rediscovered my husband. He is so happy to be alone with me that he doesn't even miss the kids!

Now I can see that the many years I gave to my kids were not in vain. Now I can say to the world: "Look out, here they come! They're going to make you better, happier, and sweeter. Why? Because they always knew they were loved." ❧

*I asked the Lord
to give me this boy, and he
has granted my request. Now
I am giving him to the Lord,
and he will belong to
the Lord his whole life.*

1 SAMUEL 1:27–28A NLT

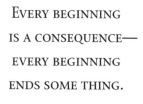

EVERY BEGINNING
IS A CONSEQUENCE—
EVERY BEGINNING
ENDS SOME THING.

PAUL VALERY

Road Curves:
Empty Nest Ahead

LYDIA E. HARRIS

That September day arrived too quickly. Our Mazda groaned under the weight of all our son's earthly possessions—French horn, computer, tennis racquet, suitcases, clothes, and snacks. The gravel crunched beneath the tires as I backed out of our driveway. We were off. I was taking our last child to college.

"Today is freedom day," I said as we drove away. "Freedom for you and freedom for me."

"I think I'll enjoy my freedom more than you will," Jonathan said, laughing.

"Why's that?" I asked.

"Any mom who cries because she no longer needs to buy two gallons of milk at once probably won't enjoy her freedom very much" he smirked.

It was true: I had cried while grocery shopping, realizing that our son wouldn't be home to drink the milk anymore. Yes, the change would be harder on me. Raising two children had kept me busy the past twenty years. Two years earlier we had taken our daughter to college. With my son gone, I faced an empty nest. How would I fill my time?

Jonathan's voice broke through my thoughts. "Are you going to cry a lot when I'm gone?"

"Maybe, but don't worry about me," I said. "I don't want you to feel responsible to make me happy. I need to get my joy from God." Verbally, at least, I tried to release him, even if a few tears betrayed me.

"Just enjoy your college years," I continued, a lump forming anew in my throat. "They pass quickly." They would for him, anyway, but would my time drag? "I remember how much fun I had in college. It's the only time in your life when you're only responsible for yourself."

Jonathan nodded and smiled. He seemed peaceful—maybe he was glad to know I didn't expect him to fulfill my needs.

The half-hour drive to Seattle Pacific University was too short. How could I shift from the past to the future in only thirty minutes?

I helped carry Jonathan's possessions into his dorm room, resisting the urge to help him unpack. He should decide which drawers would hold shirts, socks, and underwear, not me.

The room felt small to me. How would he manage, all cramped in this little space after sprawling in our five-bedroom split-level? And he would have to share it with someone he didn't even know.

I did my best to act aloof and nonchalant, but inwardly I anguished over his inevitable adjustments. Jonathan, barely eighteen, looked so young. Was he ready for this? If only we hadn't started him in kindergarten so soon. Then he'd be home for another year. Too late now.

I left his room, but I wasn't ready to leave the campus. Fortunately, the college held events for parents, giving me an excuse to linger. I listened intently as the college psychologist spoke of the changes, transitions, and new beginnings for students and parents. "Your relationship will never be the same, and it shouldn't be," he said. "When your student returns home for vacations or visits, you'll have a different relationship."

Somewhere amidst the psychologist's talk, God began speaking to my heart. *It's time to let go. Your role is different now.* I let these thoughts sink in. *If you stay in the background, I can really work in his life,* God whispered. *He'll become the man I want him to be.*

My eyes brimmed with tears as I remembered a simple wooden plaque Jonathan's Sunday school teacher had given him years earlier: "A boy is all God has with which to make a man." The words comforted me. God would work in Jonathan's life; it wasn't up to me. As best I could, I prayed and released my son to God.

I found Jonathan and said goodbye, then drove away in an empty car. I glanced into my rearview mirror and waved. The road curved, and Jonathan disappeared from view. My empty nest journey lay ahead.

At first, Jonathan called almost every afternoon, about the same time we once shared an after-school snack. I wanted to hear all about his new college life, and he seemed eager to learn about things at home. Often he said, "Things are going great!" I loved to hear the confidence in his voice. But when he sometimes sounded down, I wanted to rush over to hug him and make it all better. I wanted to somehow insulate him from any difficulties. But God cautioned: *Don't go. Let Me work in his life. Your job is to hug him through prayer.*

I stayed home and prayed, realizing Jonathan had to learn to depend more on God and less on me. We both needed to find new ways to lean on God.

As the year progressed, Jonathan became absorbed in his studies. He called less frequently and confided fewer details of his life. Gradually, I learned to accept what he willingly shared instead of prying with twenty questions. I sent care packages with homemade goodies, which made him popular in the dorm and made me feel needed. But mainly I prayed for him. Sometimes I prayed from Luke 2:52, that like Jesus, he would grow "in wisdom and stature, and in favor with God and men." My weekly prayers for him with other college moms encouraged me, and I saw God answer prayers and work in his life.

Was Jonathan right that he would enjoy his new freedom more than I would mine? Maybe at first. But as the months passed, I found joy in this new stage of life. As Jonathan gained independence and grew mature, I learned to find new avenues of fulfillment. I had time to focus on God, my husband, home, friends, and serving my church. I stayed in touch with my son by attending campus concerts and inviting his friends over for home-cooked meals. But mostly, I prayed for him and developed new interests and relationships of my own.

Looking at my son today, married and with two young children of his own, I am proud of the man I see. When I released him, God took my boy and made a godly man. ✤

*It is God who works in you both
to will and to do for His good pleasure.*

PHILIPPIANS 2:13

God's Promises for Letting Go

Even to your old age and gray hairs I am he,
I am he who will sustain you. I have made you and
I will carry you; I will sustain you and I will rescue you.

ISAIAH 46:4 NIV

Trust in the Lord with all your heart,
And lean not on your own understanding;
In all your ways acknowledge Him,
And He shall direct your paths.

PROVERBS 3:5–6

The children of Your
servants will continue,
And their descendants will
be established before You.

PSALM 102:28

For I am about to do something new.
See, I have already begun! Do you not see it?
I will make a pathway through the wilderness.
I will create rivers in the dry wasteland.

ISAIAH 43:19 NLT

*Grandchildren are the
crowning glory of the aged;
parents are the pride
of their children.*

PROVERBS 17:6 NLT

THE GIFT OF A GRANDCHILD

When we became mothers, we entered into a brand-new time in our lives. Everything was wild and wonderful. Likewise, when we become grandmothers, we experience an all-new kind of love.

There's no manual for how to be a grandma, and no one can quite explain it to you. It's really quite simple: You now have a new flock of precious little family members, and your only responsibility is to love them.

PERFECT LOVE
SOMETIMES DOES NOT
COME UNTIL THE
FIRST GRANDCHILD.

WELSH PROVERB

The Gift of My Granddaughter

BARBARA BRADLEY

Years ago, my friends told me of a love they said was completely unique—that is, those of my friends who had become grandparents. "There's nothing like it," they said. "Just you wait and see."

As a mother, I believed in the truth of the belief that there is no love like that between a mother and child. But I never really pondered the wonder of grandmother love. Becoming a grandmother was not among my future dreams; I simply couldn't envision myself in the role. I was much too young to be a grandmother, for one thing.

And then it happened.

The special bonding took place between Alicia and me when she was three days old. I kept her bassinet in my room to allow her mom and dad a good night's rest. She slept soundly until 2 A.M., a full two hours before her next feeding. When her weak little cry awakened me, I found her pacifier, placed it in her mouth, and patted her tummy. Off to sleep she was in a matter of seconds. I could hardly wait until she woke up again.

Through the years, how many similar, exquisitely beautiful moments we've shared. When she began learning to speak, the words "Grandma Barbara" were a big mouthful for the little one. I became Grandma BaBa until, gradually, she learned she could easily get my attention by referring to me as "BaBa." Dropping the "Grandma" hasn't deflected my pride in being a grandmother in the slightest. I consider the title she bestowed upon me to be the most distinguished in the world.

My late husband, Jimmy, whom she called "Pop Pop," fought a long and courageous battle with leukemia. During his illness, she would sit in the den beside his hospital bed and ask, "Can I be your nurse tonight?"

She brought him water and brushed his hair, and then we often played her favorite game, she in her role as teacher with Jimmy and me as her students.

The drives to and from school together were also special. On the first anniversary of Jimmy's death, she leaned across the seat, put her hand on my shoulder and said, "BaBa, I know this is a sad day for you. If we were home, I'd rub your back so you would feel better." No one had mentioned the significance of the date, but it was on the mind of this young child. She sensed the feelings deep inside without a word having been spoken.

During those rides through her neighborhood, we laughed, talked, and sang our favorite songs. Never mind that I was an Engelbert fan and she liked rock music. She gave me a very special affirmation of her love when she attended an Engelbert concert with me when she was twelve.

One of my prized possessions is from a fourth-grade class project. On pink construction paper, she described my favorite color, song, and tree (magnolia, planted by her Pop Pop) and how she liked going to church with me. She knew me well.

I treasure the day I knew we would never have to worry about her through the turbulent teens. During confirmation at church, she spoke of her faith in God and appreciation of family. Now a sophomore in college, her life exemplifies the same simple faith, sense, and sensibilities I've so often observed in her on her road to adulthood.

In a recent class assignment, students in her class were asked to give a presentation about their hero. Alicia told me she had named me as her hero. "I chose you, BaBa," she said. "I want to be just like you." I fought tears, humbled by the thought that I had inspired such a quality young lady, that she had seen something in me she wanted to emulate.

I reflect on her childhood, her quiet confidence and wisdom, and I remember that bond born in infancy. What kind of unconditional love is it that overlooks our flaws and imperfections, that peeks deep inside us and sees not that which we are, but that which we aspire to be?

Maybe it's a love that reaches beyond the human finite into a bit of the infinite love that God imbues on all His children. ❀

Old people are proud of their grandchildren,
and children are proud of their parents.

Proverbs 17:6 NCV

Good Days Ahead

What's the best thing about being a grandma? There are so many good things to choose from—

- You don't have to worry about spoiling the kids— spoiling is your new job description.
- Photo opportunities abound, most of which will end up on your refrigerator.
- You get all the fun of babies and kids—and you can send them home for all the diapers and tantrums.
- You have an outlet for all the wisdom you've acquired since you had kids of your own.
- Less responsibility, more fun.

Grandmotherhood is a wonderful new world. Enjoy every moment! ❀

BECOMING A GRANDMOTHER IS WONDERFUL.
ONE MOMENT YOU'RE JUST A MOTHER. THE NEXT
YOU ARE ALL-WISE AND PREHISTORIC.

PAM BROWN

WHAT A BARGAIN
GRANDCHILDREN ARE!
I GIVE THEM MY LOOSE CHANGE,
AND THEY GIVE ME A MILLION
DOLLARS' WORTH OF PLEASURE.

GENE PERRET

Grateful Grandma Gushing

ROBIN EHRLICHMAN WOODS

Call me "daughter," and I am transported back to the halcyon days of unconditional love from my mommy. Being the eldest of three girls, I am also comfortable with the title of "sister," and I've grown into the roles of wife and daughter-in-law as well. Motherhood and all its blessings are right up my alley, and my sweet son-in-law calls me his "little Mamela."

But I have finally met my match with something so earth shattering, I cannot wrap my mind around it: I am going to be a grandmother. And suddenly, I am consumed by the ramifications of entering this stage in my life.

Oh, how I want to smell the sweetness of an infant's neck again and hear the precious mewling coos whispered from tiny doll-like lips. But somehow, I have been spending an inordinate amount of time obsessing about what I will be to my daughter's baby.

I think of "grandmas" as nurturing old ladies, whereas I have been mistaken for a well-preserved, fortyish femme fatale from time to time. "Grannies" bring to mind

crotchety, fusty, blue-haired gals in sensible shoes, while a
"Nana" is the petite woman toiling in the kitchen, making
homemade blintzes and potato latkes while saying, "Essen,
shaynah maidel." (Yiddish for "Eat, pretty girl.")

That was my sweet Nana, a title I would never claim as
my own. How could I live up to her memory?

As the months go by and my daughter's due date
approaches, I wonder whether I will ever seem young to
anyone again. There is a six-year-old inside me, trying
not to misbehave as I attempt to focus on the upcoming
miracle of my first grandchild.

I am not ready to fill in another arc in the rapidly
closing circle of life. If that's all there is, I choose to veer
off and make a hexagon instead. To ease my transitional
emotional funk, family and friends are offering suggestions
for alternate, hipper grandma names.

"The baby can call you Oma. It's German for
'Grandma.'" Oh, my. Too hausfrau and Lederhosen for me.

"My sister Kathy has her grands call her K-Ma." That
would make me R-Ma, or Ro-Ma. Next choice, please.

Worrying about my daughter's pregnancy and
delivery should be first on my list, but I am stuck on the
notion of denying and lying about the aging process. I

am fighting this crisis tooth and nail, discretion tossed to the winds.

The more my soon-to-appear grandson kicks, the closer I come to entering a fugue state. I have always looked and acted decades younger than my husband, who is more than ready to be a "Poppa." He can barely wait to unwrap one of life's most wondrous gifts. I gingerly await the newest link in our family chain as emotions tug a bit too tightly at my heart, and I know that no matter if I am a "Nana" or "Gamma," I am going to go gaga over my first grandson.

As morning sickness transcend into labor pains, I pace and chatter mindlessly during the birthing process. My baby is having a baby, but I am barred from the delivery room. Hours pass in a blur until I see my son-in-law barreling into the waiting room, photos waving aloft in his shaking hands.

Tears blur my vision as I glance at Benjamin Pax Esser for the first time. He is big and pink, an eight-pound, nine-ounce solid chubby cherub who came out screaming with anger. The obstetrician had commented that she never heard as loud a bellow from a newborn before as Benjamin stared at her, his eyes wide open from the moment he fought his way out of his tight cocoon.

I stand transfixed and press my nose up against the glass of the newborn nursery window, waiting for Benjamin's first bath and checkup. As a nurse holds him up and brings him closer for my first inspection, he peers at me calmly and intently.

We send silent messages of love back and forth as our eyes lock. My heart opens as wide as infinity in unabashed adoration over my gift, my path to immortality as the generations of our family expand on this glorious birthday.

Call me anything you want, Benjamin. I am yours forever. ❀

Where you go, I will go. Where you live,
I will live. Your people will be my people,
and your God will be my God.

RUTH 1:16B NCV

Passing the Torch

Paul wrote to his young protégé, Timothy, "I remember your true faith. That faith first lived in your grandmother Lois and in your mother Eunice, and I know you now have that same faith" (2 Timothy 1:5 ncv). Later, he affirmed that Timothy had been taught the Scriptures since he was a small boy (2 Timothy 3:15). It seems that Timothy's mother and grandmother had left him a legacy of faith.

When we become grandmas, we have the same opportunity that Timothy's grandmother had. We are able to pray for our grandkids and share Scriptures and stories with them, instilling in them the belief and confidence in God that have enriched our lives.

Being a grandma is a very special blessing. Not only do we have a new crop of kids to hug; we have the opportunity to pray for them and bless them. ❁

We will not hide them from their children,
Telling to the generation to come the praises of the Lord,
And His strength and His wonderful works that He has done.

PSALM 78:4

God's Promises
for New Beginnings

The Lord will fulfill his purpose for me;
your love, O Lord, endures forever—
do not abandon the works of your hands.

PSALM 138:8 NIV

And I am certain that God, who began the
good work within you, will continue his work
until it is finally finished on the day
when Christ Jesus returns.

PHILIPPIANS 1:6 NLT

*The Lord will guard you as you
come and go, both now and forever.*

PSALM 121:8A NCV

*He satisfies me with good things and
makes me young again, like the eagle.*

PSALM 103:5 NCV

ACKNOWLEDGMENTS

"Clothes Closet Capers" © Patricia Lorenz. Used by permission. All rights reserved.

"A Daily Dose of Miracles" © Louise Tucker Jones. Used by permission. All rights reserved.

"The Gift of My Granddaughter" © Barbara Bradley. Used by permission. All rights reserved.

"Gifts from My Baby" © Stephanie Welcher Thompson. Used by permission. All rights reserved.

"Grateful Grandma Gushing" © Robin Ehrlichman Woods. Used by permission. All rights reserved.

"The Harvest" © Karen Majoris Garrison. Used by permission. All rights reserved.

"How I Spent My Summer Vacation" © Patricia Lorenz. Used by permission. All rights reserved.

"I Couldn't Let Go of My Children, So They Let Go of Me" © Joan Clayton. Used by permission. All rights reserved.

"A Knowing Friend" © Louise Tucker Jones. Used by permission. All rights reserved.

"Mommy to You Both" © P. Jeanne Davis. Used by permission. All rights reserved.

"My Mother's Wisdom" © Amy Shore. Used by permission. All rights reserved.

"My Prodigal Son" © Nanette Thorsen-Snipes. Used by permission. All rights reserved.

"The Other Mother" © Michelle Starkey. Used by permission. All rights reserved.

"Put Your Worry Alarm on Snooze" © Margaret Lang. Used by permission. All rights reserved.

"Road Curves: Empty Nest Ahead" © Lydia E. Harris. Used by permission. All rights reserved.

"School Days" © Nancy B. Gibbs. Used by permission. All rights reserved.

"Spring Portraits" © Heather Lynn Ivester. Used by permission. All rights reserved.

"A Walk in the Park" © Patricia Lorenz. Used by permission. All rights reserved.

"The Walking Stick" © Elece Hollis. Used by permission. All rights reserved.